Born to L.E.A.D

Leveraging Efforts and Attitudes into Dreams

By

Garrett W. Milby

CONTENTS

DEDICATION

I dedicate this book to my wife Jetona, for believing in and supporting me, as I pursued my dream of writing this book. To Wesley, I hope that this book can assist you as you grow into the young man I know you will become. I love you both yesterday, today and forever.

Your Loving Husband and Father

SPECIAL THANKS

I want to thank God for all of His goodness, giving me the words, the courage, and the dedication to write this book.

A "special thanks" goes to Alison Frederick for taking the time to edit my book, Shayne Bryant at Next Level Photography in Destin, Florida for taking the photo used for the cover, and to all of my family and friends for believing in me and encouraging me through this process.

Foreword

"For I know the plans I have for you, declares the Lord, plans to prosper you and not to harm you, plans to give you hope and a future" Jeremiah 29:11. Throughout Garrett's life, even in the midst of uncertainty, trials, and tribulations, he has never given up on God's plan for him and his life. He and his life's testimony serve as a grand example of perseverance and born leadership. I am blessed to have the opportunity of knowing this man as my life partner for the past twelve years and a father to our son for the past year.

Garrett was born and raised in rural Kentucky. Growing up on a farm after having parents that divorced when he was three years old and acclimating to a blending family at age ten, Garrett became well attuned to negotiating key relationships, rising above his circumstances, and demonstrating responsibility and leadership in a variety of avenues and facets. It was evident from early on that Garrett was destined for positions in leadership, serving as defensive captain on his high school football team for several years, representing his graduating class in leadership roles, and always being the guy a friend went to for sound advice or to help solve a problem. Garrett was well-revered by his classmates and peers; and his humor, good-nature, and charismatic personality are traits that continue to follow him throughout adulthood and in his relationships today as well.

Garrett has served the majority of his professional career as a male adult mentor/role model in the capacity of leading and educating the youth of today, assisting them in discovering their true potential, identifying and using their "God gifts", and encouraging them that no dream or goal is too small for them if they aim high and maintain their faith and focus. In addition to his professional experience with children, adolescents, and young adults as a Higher Education Recruiter and Career & College Readiness Coach, Garrett also has served in our United States Armed Forces for the past eleven years and during that time has served as a leader amongst his fellow servicemen in the United States Air National Guard on several occasions during various trainings and drills.

While this book serves as an inspiring guide in navigating you through some of life's' most pivotal moments and questions, it also offers practical advice and discerning wisdom to the inquisitive and driven reader. It is my hope that while reading this thoughtfully developed piece of literature, created and designed in hope and love, you realize the genuineness and authenticity of the author's words. Above all, I desire that you uncover the natural leader inside of you and fulfill God's plan for your live as well.

Preface

As I sit in my office, surrounded by four walls, a large desk, a chair and a rectangular window, I find myself staring out into the world I once knew and once was a part of so freely. In February 2012, my family's prayers were answered. After four years of being away physically and emotionally, I received a job offer that changed our lives. The days of being gone from sunrise to sunset were over. The Saturday work was over, the missing of events and activities, over.

In March 2012, I gave up my job as an outside admissions recruiter and went into the world of office life. I left behind the long days, the constant windshield (driving) time, the numerous miles, the wear and tear on the vehicle and my body, the sell-sell-sell mentality, the haggling of bosses wanting more while giving us less to work with, the non-stop emails and text messages. I gave up the challenge.

Giving up the challenge also meant leaving behind the goal of trying to make a difference. For four years I made it a goal not to be a salesman but to be a motivator and leader. I wanted to show young adults from all walks of life that no matter what your circumstance, be it a situation, family, work or friends, they have the ability to rise above it and become more. I wanted to make a difference in the lives of young adults who were looking for someone who cared, seeking an answer to what they were going to do upon graduating from high school, or hunting for something that made sense and gave them hope.

….The day I left admissions I left apart of myself behind.

Now don't get me wrong I was happy. In fact, I was relieved, yet I was sad. I was happy, because for the past four years, I had given so much of myself to a career that had taken so much from me. Yes, the job provided for my wife and me. Yes, it allowed us to live in our hometown and afford some nice luxuries, but at what price? Looking back on it, I can see that for the past four years I had neglected so many things. I had betrayed my marriage by not being there for my wife as I should have been (emotionally, physically, or spiritually). I allowed a job to get in the way of my spiritual and personal growth. I was giving up the 10-16 hour days for a normal job 8 to 5 job. I was finally gaining time back, which I will discuss later.. Now I had the time to devote my time to things like golfing, relaxing on the couch, napping, and spending time with friends, family, and my wife; I was gaining freedom. Many would ask, "What is the problem here?" You found a solution, an answer to the question. The problem was in knowing that something more existed and finding what that something is.

My sadness came, because I remembered waking up every day with the mentality that I was going to make a difference. I delivered the same presentation and the same recruiting pitch to each family for four years with the same passion I had from day one.

While the faces changed from year-to-year, my goal and mission always remained the same, which was to make a difference. However, sitting in the world that I thought I wanted left me feeling empty and unfulfilled while wondering what I could do to find that fire that I left behind.

In retrospect, I realized that the fire is within me. My mission and goals have not changed. I still have the desire to make a difference in the lives of others and through this book I am going to LEAD.

Born to L.E.A.D is the culmination of all that pinned up positive aggression within me, that fire that I wake up with each day, and the desire and longing to make a difference in the lives of individuals in the world around me.

I ask that you take a journey with me as we look inward to ourselves and outward to those around us and find what it takes to lead and be lead. Through the words of the Bible and of great leaders from the past and present, you will find that sense of purpose within and be motivated to L.E.A.D in your daily lives. They say "the journey is not for everyone," but in my world the journey is for everyone who is willing to accept the challenge. I challenge you to devote your time into something that might make a difference in not only your life but the lives around you.

Will you accept the challenge? Can you leverage the world around you, while giving the maximum effort, changing your

attitudes, as you reach for your dreams? Will you be lead and will
you L.E.A.D?

Chapter 1

Leadership

Day 1: Introduction

My father always said, "One day son you will find your niche." These were wise words from a man I hold with such high regard and have even labeled as my hero. What I never realized is the fact that even at a young age, my niche was already there. God blessed me with a set of unique talents. The only problem, I had not discovered them yet.

*****

When I look at myself in the mirror, I do not see anything special about myself. When I look closer I see within me numerous events that have molded me and shaped me into the man I am today. Just a brief history lesson of who I am. I grew up on a farm as a rural country boy in Central Kentucky. My parents divorced when I was young. Both of my parents remarried. I have eight siblings (four sisters and four brothers). I graduated from high school, went to work, attended college, graduated, married my sweetheart, and now live an ordinary life. My life is not much different from anyone else's. Just like others, I have made decisions at certain junctures in my life that have taken me to where I am today. Just like most people, if I look back, I discovered things I would change. But, one thing I have learned is I cannot go back and change the past. What I can do is learn from the past and strive to make positive changes that will impact the future of my life, in the life of other's, and for future generations.

*****

From a very young age, I have always wanted to be in the forefront. I was never the person who tried to seek attention or needed attention, but what I wanted was to be the leader. Not in just a few things, but in all things. I have always wanted to be the go-to person. I always wanted to be the spokesman of the group. I liked it when I was charged with big responsibilities. Okay, I admit it. Deep inside of myself I have always wanted to be recognized by my peers and be the best in everything I do. It, however, was not until I started playing football in middle school that my leadership skills begin to develop. I suppose my coaches knew I had it in me, because I was placed at middle linebacker. If you did not know, being middle linebacker meant you get to lead the defense. After being placed there, I thought of all the linebackers who had or were playing that position and tried to imitate those individuals. I wanted to emulate individuals like Dick Butkus, Ray Lewis, and Brian Urlacher just a few of the great linebackers who have played or are playing in the National Football League. As the captain of the defense, it was my job to relay the play calls from the coaches and get everyone into position. It was my job to encourage or "fire" the players up and get them ready. It was my job to impart words of encouragement if anyone missed a tackle that went for a touchdown, and it was my job to celebrate with the team when we won our games. For those six years that I played middle and high school football, I felt like I could rule the world. Nothing was going to get in my way. Football was my "heaven" and my "playground."

Then reality set in, and I found myself in the real world. My childish dreams quickly became just that, dreams. Those visions faded off into a distant past, and I was left to settle for a backup plan. Maybe you start a family, go to college, get a full-time job, or do all of the above. Whatever life path people choose, we never forget moments of our past. Those moments that shaped us into the people we have or will become. We can make a decision to accept it, or we can decide to reach for and do something more.

I, being the person that I am, have made a decision to do something more. I am a firm believer that everything happens for a reason. I believe God does make us in His own image, and that He has a plan for us. Some of us will realize it early in life and some later. But at that moment, that moment when you realize what your true purpose is and what you were made for, ask yourself whether you will choose to ignore it or embrace it and become the leader that is within you?

Throughout these pages we are going to define leadership. You are going to learn how to leverage any situation for the better, refocus your efforts, shape your attitudes, and define your dreams. Because when the day comes that your life in dwindling down and you can no longer have the time to reflect on your life and make changes, how do you want to view it? How do you want people to remember you? So take a stance now and become the leader within you. As they say on the gridiron, "leave it all out there, leave nothing in the tank," and you can walk away from your life with no regrets. Will you choose to L.E.A.D?

Day 2: The Challenge

"To be successful you must accept all challenges that come your way. You can't just accept the ones you like." -Mike Gafka

The quote above rings true for many of us. We like to pick and choose situations in our lives, typically looking for the paths that provide the least resistance. I can attest first-hand to that. Throughout my life I have always looked for ways to get ahead. I have sought the easy path, but the truth is, there is no easy way.

I often hear the saying, "work smarter, not harder," and I believe we can use this wisdom to our advantage in most situations in life. But I have found that the way to the top is not by side stepping situations or taking the path of least resistance, but rather by facing them head on as they emerge. When challenged with circumstances, I choose to work smarter, because as with anything, there are numerous ways to reach an outcome. In addition, confronting situations allows us to learn and grow personally, professionally and spiritually.

Jeremiah 29:11 (New International Version) says, "For I know the plans I have for you," declares the Lord, "plans to prosper you and not to harm you, plans to give you hope and a future." This scripture, along with many others, provides me all the strength I need to face each and every positive or negative situation that I face. It is my hope that you too will use this scripture and find other verses as inspirational, motivational and empowering regardless of the situation you face.

I want to challenge you with a simple task. Take this book seriously! Challenge yourself to commit to the book and challenge yourself daily to make incremental changes in your life in order to serve as a testament to those around you. Read, not to just say you read a book, but for substance. Within these pages there is nothing too complicated to comprehend; as Sherlock Holmes would say, "It's elementary."

There are a few things I want to accomplish:

1.   I want you to grow personally. We have to grow within ourselves before making a difference around us.

2.   I want you to grow spiritually. If you have already found God in your life CONGRATULATIONS! If not, it is my hope that along the way you can find Him, because with God on your side, nothing is impossible.

3.   What I want you to gain from this is a new perspective. Realize that with a little effort and the right attitude, dreams no matter how big or small, can be obtained. You just have to keep in mind that the journey is a process. Or as I like to view life, "it's a marathon, not a sprint." Challenges will be present, occasionally those challenges will be obvious and other times you will be unsure. But stay positive and face the challenges head on. Look inward, because the mind is a powerful thing. You alone can make it happen,

but sometimes it is easier to have a support group. Try to surround yourself with positive, uplifting people who will help you tackle these situations. Remember that when all else fails, turn to God. Know that God is here and on your side. Just remind yourself that you are not alone.

Task: Take a few moments to write down a few positives about yourself. Think about your greatest strengths and weakness. In what ways can you use these to your advantage? Name some people who you can rely on such as, those individuals who possess optimistic, empowering qualities and surround yourself with these people. Positivity feeds positive results. Pray for God to give you strength to persevere through whatever life puts in your way.

"Leadership is the challenge to be something more than average"
Jim Rohn

Day 3: The Commitment

"There is a big difference between routine and commitment. Some people just do the same routine over and over again in life, some people even get better at that same routine over and over in life, but there [are] few people who commit to get to the next level."

- Coach Bill Parcells to Curtis Martin (NFL Hall of Famer)

My father-in-law and I often discuss the meaning of "Say what you mean and mean what you say." He says it means that one is only as good as his or her word. I cannot begin to count how many times I have heard him say this. He lives by this simple motto. When I say "commitment" what happens? Do you become uncertain, fearful, or possibly scared? The word commitment to many folks is a scary word. Today when we say we are going to do something or commit to something, it frequently is taken with a grain of salt. Many people will commit to something and know in the back of their minds they have no intention of following through. We feel we must commit to everything, because we are afraid of hurting someone's feelings or be viewed as a bad person for not doing something. In the world we live today, we get so caught up in so many things: our lives, other's lives, events and plans. We sometimes simply forget what we have committed ourselves to and become overwhelmed with all of our responsibilities. When that happens, we have to let something go. There is good news though, today can we learn to commit.

Take a moment and conduct an Internet search to discover how long it takes to develop a habit. Obviously you will find numerous websites. Most likely, you will find that it takes roughly 21 to 28 days to form a habit. The days and weeks are not of importance. Now I am not asking you to learn how to commit to something for 21 days right off the bat. That is not the habit that I want you to develop. The habit I want you to develop, sticking to something once you have made a commitment. Committing to an evening out with friends or to a date night with your significant other does not take long to perfect. You simply make the plans and stick to them. With a commitment, you have to "want" to do something, become motivated, have a desire, and passion, and have an at all cost mentality.

So take a moment and commit to finishing the book. They say if you write a goal down you are more likely to succeed. So right now get a calendar out and mark off 30 days. By doing this simple task you will hold yourself accountable. If you lack commitment and focus, recruit a friend to do it with you.

The great thing about the human mind is we can do anything we set our minds to. Recently, I started working out with a friend. Working out on a daily basis is not something that I love to do. However, after going in and getting my adrenaline "pumping," I found that I actually like working out. It makes me feel good. Not only that, but there are added benefits. Working out relieves stress, reduces illness, and makes you healthier. The benefits go on. I knew that being accountable to only my friend, however, would not make me go to the gym on the daily basis, because he was not around every day. I signed up for the "12 weeks to a six-pack workout program." Every four to six weeks, I report to the trainer and he takes my measurements, weighs me in, looks over my food consumption, and in general keeps me motivated. By doing that, I became accountable to myself and to the workout regimen and my trainer. I simply made a commitment to myself and my health.

Task: Commit to reading the book and applying it to your life. Find something in your life that you have been planning to do but have not committed to, and develop a plan describing how you will reach your final destination. Below, write it down and sign your name and date it. By taking these steps, you will be holding yourself accountable.

Commitment

_____

_____

_____

Signature & Date: _____

Day 4: Leadership

Quotes about Leadership

"The task of the leader is to get his people from where they are to where they have not been."- Henry Kissinger

"Great leaders are almost always great simplifiers, who can cut through argument, debate, and doubt to offer a solution everybody can understand."- General Colin Powell

"Leadership is intentional influence."- Michael McKinney

It is evident by these quotes that leadership encompasses a variety of meanings and is viewed differently to each of us.. According to Webster's Dictionary, leadership is defined as follows:

1: the office or position of a leader

2: the capacity to lead

3: the act or an instance of leading

As you can see by theses definitions, leadership has many variations that also consist of the words lead, leading, and leader. But for our purpose, we will examine leadership from the "capacity to lead" and "the act of leading."

People throughout all of history have sought out individuals who were willing to lead; and in some cases, we look for individuals who are unwilling to lead but who have leadership qualities. Now, fast forward to current day in the world in which we live today we find folks throughout the world who are looking for the next wave of great leaders to bring about change. Looking for individuals, who possess qualities and characteristics to make positive changes within communities, the government, and in the economy.

Taking on the task of being a leader is not easy, but it is not hard either. It is having the courage to make the choice to lead. It is separating right from wrong and deciding to do right even when others might think you are wrong. It's the knowing that you are standing up, when others would rather stand by and watch, later wishing they had brought about change or a solution. Do those statements make you think about some of the areas and situations in your life? They should.

What you need to know is that taking a leadership role is not just for the strong or weak, it is dual purposed and reciprocal. Indeed, being a leader allows the strong to assist and lead the weak and the weak to assist and lead the strong. What individuals need to understand is that both groups need each other. Leaders need followers, and followers need leaders. Being a leader is a huge responsibility. When the choice is made to take the reins as a leader, you are going to want to surround yourself with people who make you strive to be better. In the book of Matthew, Jesus said it best, "If the blind lead the blind, both shall fall in the ditch."

These words are very strong. Right now, things might seem hopeless in the world around you. However, if we look within ourselves and plot a course of action to bring about change, a positive change at that, it is possible to make an incremental difference.

Task: Today make a commitment to start looking for ways to lead in your life, your family's lives, and in the lives of those individuals around you. Write down ways you can make a difference. First, start by looking inwardly at yourself and then outwardly to the world around you.

Day 5: Leaders: Born, Made or Both

"Leaders are made, they are not born. They are made by hard effort, which is the price which all of us must pay to achieve any goal that is worthwhile." – Vince Lombardi

The age old question about leaders has always been. Are leaders born or are they made? Hall of Fame and Super Bowl winning coach of the Green Bay Packers, Vince Lombardi had his thoughts on this topic as have many others. My opinion; to each their own, but I encourage you to search the Internet on this topic. You will find over 180 million hits explaining how people become leaders.

But it is in my opinion that some leaders are born and some are made. Let me simplify this by providing the following example of elementary school students and leadership. If one were to examine a group of students, he or she might notice that there is always a person who stands up and moves to the forefront and takes over the role of the leader. On the other hand, there are those who will take the backseat approach and follow. There is always a child who wants to be in the front of the line leading the group to lunch, the bathroom, or another class. However, leadership qualities go beyond young children, leadership happens at every stage of life and continues in the world around us. So how at the age of five can we say someone has been taught or made into a leader? Does an individual not have some innate quality that inwardly drives them to want to lead? But who is to say that a follower in elementary school cannot become a leader later in life?

Born or made? The answer is not for me to decide. It would take weeks, months, years or maybe a lifetime to formulate answers to this discussion. For today, we are going to look at both sides.

An article written by Robert Riggio (2009) states:

To cut to the chase, the answer is: "mostly made." The best estimates offered by research is that leadership is about one-third born and two-thirds made. The job of leading an organization, a military unit, or a nation, and doing so effectively, is fantastically complex. To expect that a person would be born with all of the tools needed to lead just doesn't make sense based on what we know about the complexity of social groups and processes.

Riggio went on to further state,

Research has shown clearly that extraverts have greater leadership potential than introverts, and so did participants in our study. Except, when we looked at social skills (which we assume is a learned skill), only the socially skilled extraverts emerged as leaders. Extraversion is only an in-born leadership advantage if one also learns and develops effective communication skills.

The debate will continue and answers will evolve into the future. But simply put, people have in born and learned qualities about them that will allow them to lead individuals and groups.

When it comes down to it, leadership is a skill that needs to be honed and practiced just like any other skill set. As a leader, a person needs to constantly be thinking of ways that he or she can strive to become better and continuously provide leadership to those who follow them. Just like wolves in the wild, when that moment of weakness shows within the leader, another pack member will challenge that leadership, looking to replace the pack leader.

Task: Thoughtfully consider whether leaders are born or made. Are you a born leader, made leader, or a little of both? What in born qualities do you possess, and what qualities have you learned that can be refined so that you can become the leader that's within you?

Day 6: Believe

"Keep your dreams alive. Understand to achieve anything requires faith and belief in yourself, vision, hard work, determination, and dedication. Remember all things are possible for those who believe."- Gail Devers

So far I have presented you with a challenge, asked you to make a commitment and started laying the ground foundation of what leadership is about. The past five days have been tough and possibly a little grueling. Starting anything, especially trying to make a positive change is not an easy task. That is where believing in oneself and cause(s) comes into play. There is nothing too complicated about believing in yourself. The complication occurs when you hear from those around you who do not believe in you and doubt everything you set your mind to accomplish. When you set out on the course to change within, your views, goals, and dreams, be sure to surround yourself with those positive, uplifting individuals, because you need people who will believe in you and provide positive, encouraging feedback.

How does one go about making positive changes in beliefs? I have four thoughts on the matter, but many more ideas on this topic exist.. Yet, these four jump out to the front of my mind.

1.   It all starts with believing in YOU. M.Farouk Radwan once wrote,

Billions of people fail to live the life they have always wished to live. They fail to realize their ambitions and give up on their big dreams as soon as they encounter the first obstacle. One of the strongest causes for this attitude is that they do not believe in themselves.

2.   People follow those they believe in.

If you believe in yourself others will start to believe in you. Face the opposition, knock down their negativity and keep pressing onward. Some people are skeptical. They want to believe but cannot until they see some change or results. So keep pushing onward and prove to people you are what you say you are.

3.   Do not worry with what people think of you.

This is the hardest thing for me to accept. My need and want to have everyone believe in me comes at a price, as I fear what others think and being rejected.

Some people think that unless everyone agrees with them then they are wrong. This is completely wrong. No one ever succeeds without being rejected. If people think that you are wrong or that your efforts will yield no results, then just go against them by either convincing them with your point of view right away or by waiting until they believe in you by force when they see your success.(Radwan)

4.   Seek strength from God

You have learned that no matter what situation that you find yourself in, you always have someone there who believes in YOU. Although you may think God is not visible at all times, He is. And, at a moment's notice, you have a direct communication line to Him. Use it. You will need spiritual strength and guidance along your journey.

Mark 5:36 But overhearing what they said, Jesus said to the ruler of the synagogue, "Do not fear, only believe."

Task: Challenge your beliefs. Find ways to erase negativity and fear and replace it with positivity and bravery. What do you believe strongly in? Have you had any dreams or goals that you wanted to accomplish only to have them "rejected"? Today dust those ideas off, breathe life back into them and pursue your dreams, goals and aspirations. You never know what might come from a rebirth.

Day 7: Rest

So God blessed the seventh day and made it holy, because on it God rested from all his work that he had done in creation.   -
Genesis 2:3

God worked hard for six days and rested on the seventh. So should you. Take time to rest your mind. Do something you enjoy. Spend time with family or friends. Read a book. Take a nap. It is your day to do with as you please.

Just like working out at the gym, the body needs rest, and your mind needs to rest too.

A few encouraging words:

Here is to you. You made it!!! One week down, and only three more to go. Do you have it in you? Remember to challenge yourself and make the commitment to follow through. Your efforts and attitudes will carry you to your dreams. Keep up the good work and together we will make it.

Task: Reflect on the past week and write down any answers to the following questions. Do you see any differences in your thinking? What challenges have you faced? Are there areas that you are growing? Areas you are falling behind in? Any questions, comments or concerns? Keeping a journal will allow you to go back and see how you are progressing.   Stay positive, be optimistic, and continue to strive for better.

Comfort Zone

Author Unknown

I used to have a comfort zone where I knew I wouldn't fail.
The same four walls and busy work were really

more like jail.
I longed so much to do the things I'd never done before,
But stayed inside my comfort zone and paced the same old floor.

I said it didn't matter that I wasn't doing much.
I said I didn't care for things like commission checks and such.
I claimed to be so busy with things inside my zone,
But deep inside I longed for something special of my own.

I couldn't let my life go by just watching others win.
I held my breath; I stepped outside and let the change begin.
I took a step and with new strength I'd never felt before,
I kissed my comfort zone goodbye and closed and locked the door.

If you're in a comfort zone, afraid to venture out,
Remember that all winners were at one time filled with doubt.
A step or two and words of praise can make your dreams come true.
Reach for your future with a smile; Success is there for you!

CHAPTER 2

LEVERAGE

Day 8: Accomplishment

One of our greatest strengths is our mind. If you think you can, then you can. –Former Teacher

Leverage can be looked at in numerous ways. How I want you to view it is from the perspective of the ability to accomplish or get something done. You have made it through one week of reading. Did you ever think you would do that? Already, you have accomplished something even when I challenged your thinking and asked you to make a commitment. Here you are at week two and moving forward. As we progress, it is time to start looking at what you are going to accomplish.

There is no time to turn back. You have set a goal(s), and you are working toward them. Today is a pivotal time, because it is much like making a commitment to working out. The first week is the easy one. In week two, we generally begin to slack off, because we are sore, weak, or broken. We tell ourselves that we can do it, but it is too hard. I am not the right person. Simply put, I cannot do it. But now is the time to find that inner strength and move forward. Now is the time to say, I can do it. I will accomplish it. I will make a difference. Whatever your goal(s), dream(s) or passion , set your mind toward accomplishing them. As one of my teachers use to say,

"One of our greatest strengths is our mind. If you think you can, then you can."

What is it that you want to accomplish in your life, school, career, family, or in the world around you? Do you strive for something more? Every person has the ability to make a difference in some capacity whether it be good or bad. Some individuals are more motivated than others, but we all have something we want to accomplish. Just like a heat-seeking missile, we have to aim, lock and engage. Maybe you have some goals or dreams such as wanting to graduate high school, become a first generation college graduate, start a business, or discover something that is life changing. My question is what is stopping you? It is good to have all of these small goals and desires. However, we have to set a course to accomplish what we set out to do.

After high school, I tried the whole college scene. I thought I was committed to my education, but I quickly realized that working, making money, doing other things were more important and putting time into studying was not for me. If that was not enough evidence, my 2.5 grade point average was. My priorities were not where they needed to be. So I made the decision, after my first semester, to withdrawl from school and focus on a career. However, my turning point came after working in the warehouse industry for about three years and having an in depth conversation with my friend who said, "You're smart. You have abilities. Do not be like me and end up here for the next 16 years of your life." At that moment, I realized there was something more. I realized that I was short changing myself and my abilities. Then in May of 2005, I made the decision to return to college. My motivation was that I wanted to prove not only to myself, but everyone, that I could do it. As with any larger task, I started with a small goal to obtain an associate's degree. While attending school, I made it a goal to strive to earn A's in all of my classes. After getting rewarded with a few A's, it became motivation to continue to get more. I quickly realized that education was not only educational, but it was fun. So, before graduating with my associate's degree, I made another commitment, which was to earn a bachelor's degree. Then in December 2008, my goals and dreams paid off as I walked across the stage, shook hands, and accepted my degree in front of my family. All the hard work and dedication paid off. My dream of obtaining my degree became a reality.

The main point to my story is that we can accomplish anything we set our minds to, or we can make as many excuses possible not to. We can say "Well I do not have the money, I do not have the support system," or "No one cares," etc. But until we start believing in ourselves and our own abilities, we have no one to blame but ourselves.

Task: I want you to take a moment and consider your goals and dreams. After thinking about them, start developing a plan to accomplish them. As Stephen Kaggwa stated, "Try and fail, but don't fail to try."

Day 9: Fear

"Our deepest fear is not that we are inadequate. Our deepest fear is that we are powerful beyond measure. It is our light, not our darkness, that most frightens us. Your playing small does not serve the world. There is nothing enlightened about shrinking so that other people won't feel insecure around you. We are all meant to shine as children do. It's not just in some of us; it is in everyone. And as we let our own lights shine, we unconsciously give other people permission to do the same. As we are liberated from our own fear, our presence automatically liberates others" –Marianne Williamson

From the first time I heard this quote after watching the movie Coach Carter, it has stuck with me. Why do we fear so much? I personally have allowed fear to place restraints in my life. I was asked once "What is your biggest fear?" I responded "Not being good enough and success."

I have realized that though we all fear something. Fear typically starts at a young age with monsters in the closet or under our beds. Our imagination conjures up fears of snakes and spiders. As we grow, our fears change and we may fear that people will leave us. All of these fears are understandable. But we cannot let our fears turn into phobias that hinder our life. My question is why do we fear at all? Why not strive to be more than we are? Why not allow ourselves to be great?

Isaiah 41:10 says "Fear not, for I am with you; be not dismayed, for I am your God; I will strengthen you, I will help you, I will uphold you with my righteous right hand."

This passage alone should give you the strength that you need to be brave and fear nothing. We manifest fear throughout our lives. We fear that we will never be good enough, or we will remain inadequate. We fear rejection of our thoughts and ideas. We fear rejection in love and careers. Throughout history, there are great stories of men and women who looked fear in the eye, stared it down and overcame it.

• In the American Revolution, America wanted freedom from Britain's rule. The task was not easy, war ensued, and in the end America accomplished its goal and became independent.

• After years of violence and being enslaved, Harriet Tubman fled slavery and never returned. She made it her mission along with the Underground Railroad to assist in freeing as many slaves from the South as possible.

• You had and have fears. Maybe you are struggling with them now, maybe you have overcome them. Do not stop facing them. Become a master of your fears.

Overcoming fear is, well, fearful. Due to the world we live in and the negative thinking in our lives, many of us believe we cannot do something. I think it is time to start believing that we can. It is in my opinion that fear should not be something that holds us back or brings us down, settling for less and becoming complacent where we are. Fear should be used as a positive, motivating force for the betterment of us and the world around us. Fear should be used to drive us and motivate us to overcome whatever challenges, obstacles or circumstance stands in our way of where or who we want to be. Do not let fear become your disability or crutch. Use fear to strengthen your mind and help you face situations and obstacles. Harness your fear and turn it into a positive force.

Task: Fear is a scary word. What does fear mean to you? What fears do you have? Are there fears that you need to face and overcome? How can or will you face the fears using them to strengthen you and not allow fears to take over your life?

Day 10: Adversity

"Adversity has the effect of eliciting talents which, in prosperous circumstances, would have lain dormant." -Horace

I want to be blunt for a moment. We all face adversity. But as Disraeli put it, "There is no education like adversity." Adversity is considered to be a misfortune or unfavorable event. I say adversity by definition is a bad thing, but we can transform it into a good thing. When faced with adversity, we are the architects, the master craftsmen. It is up to us to build it into what we want it to be. We can either choose to overcome it or become oppressed by it.

Below are a few stories of individuals, who when faced with adversity, overcame it and turned those situations into positive outcomes:

• Growing up in poverty in Mississippi, she overcame sexual abuse as a child. At the age of 14, she lost a child to death. She leveraged her adversity into a talk show and became a media mogul. Today she is one of the richest women of all time. Oprah Winfrey (Academy of Achievement)

• In 1882 she fell ill and became deaf, blind and mute. She graduated from college in 1904, cum laude. In 1920 she helped co-found the American Civil Liberties Union (ACLU) and became one of the 20th century's leading humanitarians. Helen Keller (Biography.com)

•   In the late 1990's Matt Redman's hometown church was having a dry spell with their praise and worship. The Soul Survivor church located in Watford, England decided to get rid of their high tech sound equipment for a season. The song Heart of Worship was born (Welles).

Adversity is not a coincidence. God placed adversity in our lives so we could recognize areas in our lives that we are weak. After recognizing our weakness, we seek Him, as He will supply our every need. Adversity allows us to grow and learn. In addition to growing, we also learn to lean on and become dependent upon God, finding strength and courage to face any situation that life puts in our way.

As Matthew 6:33 says "But seek first His kingdom and His righteousness, and all these things will be given to you as well."

Adversity can be classified as a fear. But we have the capability to overcome fears. In life we all have struggles, obstacles, and road blocks that seem to restrain us, such as, the loss of a loved one, divorce, failed relationships, being bullied, and things that render us helpless and thinking there is no resolution to the matter. But the truth is that we can find strength within ourselves, find assurance from friends and family, and when all else fails turn it over to God, letting Him assist us in the ways that He deems best.

I have never been told life would be easy. Come to think of it, I have always been told that it only gets harder as we assume more responsibilities such as jobs, bills, marriage, and children, just to name a few. However, when we seek the Lord, become obedient to Him, cast our fears on Him, He in return will deliver us.

Task: What types of adversity are you currently facing in your life? How is it hindering you? How can you leverage these adverse situations and turn it into a positive outcome for your life?

Remember that when all else fails, cast your problems on God. He is here to help. If you open your heart and mind to Him, He will guide your way.

After watching and listening many times to Curtis Martin's induction speech into the National Football League Hall of Fame, I encourage you to listen to it. His transformation from childhood to what he has become now is truly inspiring.

Verse: "Cast all your anxiety on Him for He cares for you" 1 Peter 5:7

Day 11: Compromise

"If you just set out to be liked, you would be prepared to compromise on anything at any time, and you would achieve nothing."- Margaret Thatcher

If you take the time to research history, you will find that almost everything that has been accomplished has resulted from compromise.

•   1787-The Great Compromise brought about a resolution as it related to representation of the people purposed in The Virginia Plan and The New Jersey Plan.

•   1850-Five laws were constructed, presented, and passed to deal with issues of slavery.

By now most of us know the difference between right and wrong. Yet, we continue to get placed in some very difficult situations in life, such as, situations where we have to make decisions, which are sometimes easy, but often difficult. When faced with decisions, we have to make a choice. As with any choice, there are always two outcomes: positive or negative. When making decisions that relate to only ourselves, we typically choose the one that is in our best interest or we add a couple of friends and increase the peer pressure, and we find ourselves compromising our positions and stances.

In this day and age when life seems to be more difficult than ever, having to face more obstacles, and having no mental clarity about anything, compromise tends to be the solution and answer to everything. I am not going to say that compromising is a bad thing. I just feel that with many things we lack the mental clarity to see things from a futuristic standpoint and concentrate too much on the here and now. There are several situations such as: where to eat, what clothes to wear, what to do this weekend that compromise usually works in a positive result. Then there are the moments when we face extreme adversity: going to a party where there is alcohol, not telling the truth, allowing things to happen that you know are not right.

One of the biggest problems facing the world today is not just economic hardships or loss of jobs and homes. Rather, one of the biggest issues, is that people have lost their stance on doing what is right – their moral compasses are out of synch. We have lost ethical principles. Many people have adopted the mentality that is not their place or not their problem or issue; therefore, they decide to do nothing. We have compromised by failing to do what is right or decided not to do anything at all. I have heard countless stories from older generations of how today is nothing like when they were growing up. I enjoy listening to stories of days of old when people helped their neighbors, stopped to assist in changing a tire, gave someone a ride, gave money to assist individuals in need, gave their time and energy freely to help out in anyway, without ever once thinking about what's in it for me.

As we fast forward to today I ask where is this neighborly love, what happened to all the kindness, efforts and attitudes of individuals that filled the hearts and minds of so many? When did we start losing our moral and ethical principles? The problem in my opinion is we started compromising what is right and slowly turned to the not doing anything at all mentality.

From today forward take a stance in your life to stand for what is right even when it seems like everyone is against you. My advice to you is to stop compromising who you are, your views, your goals and dreams. When it is all said and done those individuals who pushed you and persuaded you to compromise your position will be nowhere to be found. However, I can promise you this, the whole world might not be standing behind you or beside you but there is someone much stronger and powerful that will always stand with you.

Task: What areas in your life have you compromised your position? How can you start to stand for what is right while facing the ridicule of others?

Verse: Joshua 1:9 "Have I not commanded you? Be strong and courageous. Do not be frightened, and do not be dismayed, for the Lord your God is with you wherever you go."

Day 12: Overcoming

"The truth is that our finest moments are most likely to occur when we are feeling deeply uncomfortable, unhappy, or unfulfilled. For it is only in such moments, propelled by our discomfort, that we are likely to step out of our ruts and start searching for different ways or truer answers."-M. Scott Peck

Simply put, we face many challenges in life. No one is immune to such circumstances. Unfortunately, no one knows what you are facing if those circumstances are left unknown. However, it is in those moments of adversity, challenge and obstacles that we define who we are, what we will become and where we will go. We can sit all day thinking about the whys. Why me? Why now? Why did it happen? But what if we turn that negative talk into positive talk and address it by asking ourselves different questions. Why not me? Why not now? When we begin looking at barriers from a different perspective, changing negatives into positives, it is only then that we will truly start to understand what is in store for our lives.

I recently came across a story written by Paulo Coelho. He puts overcoming things of our lives into perspective in the following story:

A famous Sufi master was invited to give a course in California. The auditorium was full at 8 a.m., which was the time it had been announced that it would begin.–At that moment, one of the assistants came onto the stage. "The master is just waking up, please be patient."

Time passed, and people started leaving the room. At midday, the assistant returned to the stage, saying that the master would be starting the lecture the minute he finished talking to a pretty girl he had just met. Most of the remaining audience left.

At 4 p.m. the master appeared - apparently drunk. This time, all but six people stormed out. "I will teach you this" said the master, ceasing to act drunk, "Whoever wishes to go down a long path, must learn that the first lesson is to overcome early disappointments."

The final statement, "the first lesson is to overcome early disappointments" is very true in each of our lives. We have all faced disappointments in life. I can recall on several occasions while playing football, looking into the stands trying to find my father and for reasons unknown at the time he would not be there. While I was disappointed, I never quit or gave up. My teammates relied on me and I had a family right there on the field with me.

No matter what age you are, you have or will face disappointments. Unfortunately, that is the sad truth. Just take a moment and look around. You can find disappointment all around. Our friends and family have let us down. Maybe we didn't get the job that we wanted. Perhaps relationship failed. Possibly we did not get the grade we thought we would get, or maybe you didn't get accepted to the college you had your heart set on. But it is in these moments that we have to overcome our shortcomings and make the best of each situation. While overcoming disappointment is never easy, we have to adopt a mindset that if one door closes, another one will open. Usually the door that opens is actually better than we had imagined. In addition, we can find strength in knowing that God has a plan, and He knows what we need at that exact moment in our lives.

Task: Think about some disappointments you have experienced and are currently dealing with. Now take time to overcome the shortcomings that you have been or are facing. Know that you can cast your problems on God and find strength in Him, that His plan is better than our plan.

Verse: Accept the following motto: Luke 6:31: "And as you wish that others would do to you, do so to them."

Day 13: Influence

"Think twice before you speak, because your words and influence will plant the seed of either success or failure in the mind of another." - Napoleon Hill

I openly express to those closest to me that when I leave this Earth, I want someone to stand up as they are delivering my eulogy and say all the things expected, such as, I was a loving husband, father, son, and devoted Christian. But I also hope that they can honestly say that I made a difference and positively influenced the lives of those around me. I have this sense of paying it forward. Not because I have too, but because so many people have played an influential role in my life, and it only seems right that I might be able to assist in influencing someone else.

Who or what influences you? Is it your parents, grandparents, aunts and uncles, teachers, athletes, grades, books, or groups of friends, I could go on, but I assume you get the point. These are typically the individuals or things that influence our lives. Notice I did not state whether those influences were negative or positive, because either can be true when it comes to being influenced. For most of us though, influencing will come from individuals around us.

I would like to share just a few of the influences in my life:

• My wife: She is a daily reminder to me, to be a better man, husband and father. She is my better half and my best friend. She holds me accountable to be the leader of our family. She has always seen the best in me even when I did not see it in myself. She has always encouraged and supported me in my every endeavor. She has given me guidance and most importantly remained the solid rock in my foundation.

• My brother: My brother is one of the most creative, funny, and quick-witted individuals you will ever meet, and he is only 19 years old. There are several reasons that I consider him a great influence but I will highlight only the most important. He has an unwavering respect and commitment to his faith. From a young age he clung to his spirituality and never veered. Watching him only made me want to be and do better. This alone speaks volumes, considering all the negativity that young adults face these days.

• My Granny: She is one of the hardest working women I have ever met. Not only because she has done for all of us on so many occasions and given so freely of her time, money, and effort while never asking or expecting anything in return. While being so influential in our families lives is great, she has done it all while battling an autoimmune disease called Scleroderma (a group of diseases that causes skin and sometimes internal organs to become hard and tight), and she has to my knowledge never once complained, used it as a crutch or asked why me. She just keeps enjoying her life and the blessings that have been bestowed upon her.

While these individuals influence me, I hope that in some way I influence them too. Influence is often a reciprocal relationship. We are influenced by some individual or group and, in return, we influence them and potentially others (seed planting). One of the most important things to remember, as my Granny would say, "Be careful of your actions and words, because you never know who might be watching or listening."

Task: Think about how you have been influenced by individuals and situations in your life. Now, how can you also influence individuals and situations in your life for the better? Lastly, think about one person who has been influential in your life and take time to seek them out and say thank you. You will never know what that might mean to them at that very moment.

Verse: "You are the light of the world. A city set on a hill cannot be hidden." Matthew 5:14

Day 14: Rest

WOW!!!! We have accomplished the first two weeks of the journey. Our final destination is still distant, but daily it draws closer. You must stay strong, wash away the negative mindsets and continue to develop and reinforce your positive thinking. This week touched upon some very serious issues. How are you feeling? Has it been a challenge to find the time to devote to reading? Has the commitment proven too hard?

Now is the time to drop your anchor and hold tight. YOU CAN DO THIS! As we move forward, we are going to look at how our efforts and attitudes can make a difference in our lives and potentially the lives of those around us. In addition, examining how we can start to take those baby steps to make changes in ourselves which will bring about changes outwardly. So, take a deep breath, relax, as you are going to need it.

Task: As with every rest day, I encourage you to do something fun today. Go see a family member or friend who you have not seen in a while. Take a walk in the park. Drive around with the windows down. Enjoy the day you have been blessed with. Reflect on the last two weeks and gain strength from it, as we have dealt with some very difficult issues that face each of us. Remember this is a marathon and not a sprint. You are slowly growing in your own way. Just remember practice, pace, and endurance will lead us to the finish line.

Chapter 3

Efforts and Attitudes

Day 15: Efforts and Attitudes

> "There are two things in life over which we have complete
> control...effort and attitude." - Chuck Wilson

Effort and attitude can take you a long way in this life. With the right mindset, you can accomplish just about anything. It is true that you will have to face obstacles and challenges along the way, but by having these two things inline, your success is beyond measurable. The main thing is to find a healthy balance between the two.

Before we can truly start to talk about effort and attitude, a better understanding of both is needed:

Effort, according to the Merriam-Webster Dictionary, is defined as: 1) a conscious exertion of power: hard work, 2) a serious attempt, 3) something produced by exertion or trying, and 4) the total work done to achieve a particular end.

Attitude is defined by the Merriam-Webster Dictionary as: 1) a mental position with regard to a fact or state, 2) a feeling or emotion toward a fact or state, 3) an organismic state of readiness to respond in a characteristic way to a stimulus, and 4) a: a negative or hostile state of mind *b*: a cool, cocky, defiant, or arrogant manner.

Pat Riley, a Basketball Hall of Famer once stated, "If you have a positive attitude and constantly strive to give your best effort, eventually you will overcome your immediate problems and find you are ready for greater challenges." I think with all the success Riley had over his years in basketball, we can conclude that he might be on to something. Positive attitudes will lead us to putting forth our best efforts.

I see effort and attitude in two scientific terms, mutualism and parasitic. Effort and attitude can benefit from the other or one can benefit while the other suffers. If our attitude is positive, we tend to give maximum effort. If we are giving maximum effort and seeing results, then our attitude is usually positive. When, however, we give our maximum effort and do not see the desired results, our attitude can negatively be affected, allowing us to become discouraged and displeased.

For those who prefer a visual perspective, let us relate effort and attitude to a vehicle. When everything is in order from a mechanical standpoint, for example, we get maximum performance from our vehicles. On the other hand, when the slightest problems exist, then the performance generally will suffer significantly. This is true in our everyday life. When everything around us is going well, we feel unbreakable, untouchable. We have that "I rule the world" mentality. But throw in a minor setback, any type of negative disruption, and we quickly lose that attitude and slowly stop giving our best efforts -just like the car, we start to slowly come to a complete stop.

Task: Think about your efforts and attitudes. Do they measure up to where you want them to be? Are they mutually benefiting one another or is one benefiting while the other slowly suffers? How can you take ownership of your efforts and attitudes so that you reflect positivity to those around you?

Day 16: Effort

"Winning is not everything, but the effort to win is."- Zig Ziglar

My father always taught me that the right attitude will take you far in life, but working hard (effort) will take you further. Looking back on his advice and where I am today in my life, I believe his insights were spot on. I feel that our attitudes shift daily though. We face so many things in life - both positive and negative. I believe it is only fair that we get a pass on our moods. However, what I do not believe to be true is the effort we exert, because our efforts will allow us to win in this game of life.

Each day that we wake up, we are faced with life challenges that can be dealt with in many different ways. We get to choose to embrace, deflect, or become overwhelmed by the challenges. The point is that our attitudes will reflect these moments at that specific time in our life. However, the effort in which we go about facing each day should stay the same. National Basketball Association great Larry Bird once said, "I've got a theory that if you give 100 percent all of the time, somehow things will work out in the end." We need to get in the mindset that no matter what life puts in our path, we are going to give the most of ourselves and give maximum effort to deal with each situation.

I have read countless stories, watched numerous shows and movies, of how people have been faced with what seemed like insurmountable difficulties. Such things as: death around them, homelessness, sexual abuse, failed relationships, lack of mental strength, etc. But the underlying theme to all those stories is those individuals overcame each and every obstacle. Why? Because of the effort they put into overcoming those situations. While no story is the same, the constant in each is the hardships and struggles that each individual or group faced and how they slowly overcame the situation they were faced with. What that tells me is that with a little effort we all have the ability to overcome what was behind us and what lies ahead. The main thing, when we face these situations in life; is to keep going, keep giving our best, and never quit, because the journey might be long but the good news is, there is an end in sight.

Task: Have you been giving your all? Do you know what your best is? Take a moment to jot down areas in your life in which you have been giving your all - your best effort. Now write down areas that you have been slacking in. Come up with a plan and set goals describing how you are going to give more effort to those areas in your life that you have been giving so little. You just might surprise yourself with your results.

Verse: 1 Corinthians 10:13 No temptation has overtaken you that is not common to man. God is faithful, and he will not let you be tempted beyond your ability, but with the temptation he will also provide the way of escape, that you may be able to endure it.

Day 17: Attitude

"Nothing can stop the man with the right mental attitude from
achieving his goal; nothing on earth can help the man with
the wrong mental attitude."- Thomas Jefferson

Attitude is everything. I am not sure attitudes can be
measured fairly due to the fact that everyone has and is entitled to
their opinions. I do believe that no matter how much effort you give,
that if your attitude is not right, everything else will falter. Attitudes
can make or break a person. In my life, I have heard more often
people discuss and talk about a person's attitude than any other
attribute you associate with an individual. While I do believe that
effort can take you very far in life, our attitudes tend to overshadow
any work that we have put in.

While being in the educational recruiting world for several
years, I would receive references for students from their teachers and
peers. Countless times, I heard people describe individuals in the
following ways: "they are a team player", "they are well organized",
"have time management skills", and the list continues. But one thing
that always seemed to stay constant in discussions of perspective
students was attitudes. It amazed me how the person giving the
references would openly discuss the attitudes of those they were
providing references for. Teachers would say things like "Well I
want to give you my best individuals, because I know how they act.
And if they act this way here, then they will act this way there." Or

they would simply state, "Great student, has potential, but his/her attitude is horrible." If a teacher will openly describe a person this way, it makes you wonder how others are viewing you. Simply put, attitudes matter. Attitudes can leave a person with a very positive or negative perception of someone, especially when it comes to educational or career opportunities.

In the game of life I believe our attitudes take one of two paths. We can project or be viewed as either positive or negative. We as humans have choices over how we will view events and people. Simply stated, we can control our minds, and we can choose how we project ourselves. Depending how we handle these situations, it may affect how others will view us.

Michael Phelps, at the 2012 Olympics, became the most decorated Olympian of all time. However, a lot of controversy surrounded Mr. Phelps from an attitude standpoint. His teammates, openly questioned his efforts in preparation for the past Olympics, saying things like "He doesn't train," or "He has God gifted ability and doesn't realize it or accept his gifts." They paint a picture of someone who has an attitude problem. Personally, I do not know Michael Phelps and I am not qualified to judge him, as I only see what the media wants me to see or hear. But when you hear and read things like this, your views can easily be persuaded. I can see where being the most decorated Olympian ever, could lead some into labeling him as cocky or arrogant. But then again, I can see where having obtained all the achievements, can lead to having a self-confidence that is unmatched by any other. Considering he has been so dominate in the swimming world for so many years, it's easy to see why some might view him from a negative or positive perspective.

Consider the following story about attitudes:

There once was a woman who woke up one morning, looked in the mirror, and noticed she had only three hairs on her head.

'Well', she said, 'I think I'll braid my hair today?'

So she did and she had a wonderful day.

The next day she woke up, looked in the mirror and saw that she had only two hairs on her head.

'H-M-M,' she said, 'I think I'll part my hair down the middle today?'

So she did and she had a grand day.

The next day she woke up, looked in the mirror and noticed that she had only one hair on her head.

'Well,' she said, 'today I'm going to wear my hair in a ponytail.'

So she did and she had a fun, fun day.

The next day she woke up, looked in the mirror and noticed that there wasn't a single hair on her head.

'YEA!' she exclaimed, 'I don't have to fix my hair today!'

Attitude is everything.

Author Unknown

Task: Remember, attitudes reflect the choices we make about how we will live each day. Attitudes are demonstrated, through decisions and situations that we face. Make a choice today to be positive. Allow yourself to project a positive attitude to all those around you. How does this make you feel? How do others feel about you?

Day 18: Failure

"I can accept failure. Everyone fails at something. But I can't accept not trying." -Michael Jordan

Like him, love him or hate him, Michael Jordan knows a little bit about failure. I am sure by now, you have heard the story that Michael Jordan was cut from his varsity high school team and relegated to the junior varsity squad. It has been said, that he was so upset by it that he went home and cried afterwards. Instead of giving up and accepting defeat, Michael Jordan went on to become one of the best, if the not the best, NBA basketball player of all time. As his career was coming to a close, Nike ran an ad that had the following quote

"I've missed more than 9,000 shots in my career. I've lost almost 300 games. Twenty six times I've been trusted to take the game winning shot and missed. I've failed over and over and over in my life. And that's why I succeed!" –Michael Jordan

These are some powerful words from one of the all-time greats.

In our life, it is a given, that we will try things and at some, we will succeed and at others, we will fail. However, it is the choices that we make after experiencing successes or failures that leads us forward or backward. It is in these moments, that we define who we are, who we will or will not become, and how we will be viewed. When we succeed, we are happy, excited, and feel as if we can take on and conquer the world. We believe that nothing can hold us back. But with failure, we tend to dwell on it and ponder whether there were things we could or should have done differently to bring about more desirable results. Sometimes we become complacent with the outcome, letting it negatively affect us. Or we choose to learn from it, make positive strides to become better, and create success for our futures. The choice is ours and ours alone.

I will be one of the first to admit that my competitive, overachieving mindset can be my downfall. As a child I hated to lose. Actually I was such a bad sport that my family would constantly tell me, "If I could not act any better than that, then they would never play with me again." Some harsh spoken words if you ask me, especially when you're a child. Little did I know that it was from failure that I would learn how to be a good sport. Despite the outcome, I learned that even in losses, I could still win. Sounds ridiculous I know, but I won because I knew that if as long as I gave it my all, my best efforts, then I could leave any game, event, or life situation, with my head held high.

Life is much like the games we have played throughout our lives. In the beginning, it's all about how many times we tally wins over losses. Then, slowly, as we grow and mature we realize that it is not so much about the wins or losses that matter, but rather it reflects the efforts that you put into it and the attitudes that we project from it, which will lead to our successes and not our failures.

Task: How have failures affected your life? Has failures brought about any successes? Do you still tally wins and losses? What can you do to bring about positive outcomes when failures have fallen upon your life? Remember failures are going to happen, but it is how we respond that becomes the success.

Byron Katie once said "You can have anything you want in life if you are willing to ask 1,000 people for it."

Day 19: Can Do or Will Do

"The longer I live, the more I realize the impact of attitude on life. Attitude, to me, is more important than facts. It is more important than the past, the education, the money, than circumstances, than failure, than successes, than what other people think or say or do. It is more important than appearance, giftedness or skill. It will make or break a company... a church... a home. The remarkable thing is, we have a choice everyday regarding the attitude we will embrace for that day. We cannot change our past... we cannot change the fact that people will act in a certain way. We cannot change the inevitable. The only thing we can do is play on the one string we have, and that is our attitude. I am convinced that life is 10% what happens to me and 90% of how I react to it. And so it is with you... we are in charge of our Attitudes."-Charles Swindoll

"Can you do this for me?" I hear my wife in the background, asking me to assist with one of her tasks. My simple reply, "Yes I can." She replies "Well I know you can, but will you?" I believe this example speaks boldly in everyone's life. It's no secret we can do just about anything we set our minds to do. The Bible in Philippians 4: 13 says, "I can do all things in Christ who strengthens me" which is very encouraging. But for those of us who believe we do not need any assistance or help, I am here to tell you that everyone can do something, but the real question is will you do it?

I feel that simply saying I can only answers the question. Saying "I can" never really gives that commitment to a person(s) or task(s). But saying I will, goes further, it takes an extra effort, acknowledges and commits to it. Saying I will, leads to action and makes things happen. So which will you become?

As I have previously highlighted in Day 17, I have done several interviews with potential college applicants. What many of those applicants did not know was the fact that I did reference checks on them before hand, with teachers and school administrators. What I found was that many of them had the same response about individuals. However, one of the main responses I heard was "They have a "can do" attitude." My follow up response always was "Having a can do attitude is great. But will they do it?" Many employers say they look for people who have "can do" attitudes. Why not look for people who have "a will" to do? As a person who was trying to change lives, the last thing I ever wanted, was to send someone off to college, having them invest their money and their family's money into something, but never have the will to do what is asked of them or the will to finish the goals they set.

Still to this day I remember one of my first lessons on the word "can." As a middle school student, I asked my teacher "Can I go to the restroom?" She replied "Well I do not know, can you?" They even told me "Go back to your seat and come up with a different way of asking the question." Now for anyone who has needed to use the restroom, having to go and rethink your question

64

can be quite a feat. So after moments of deliberation within, I figured out that the proper question was "May I". I was applauded by my teacher and awarded permission to go to the restroom.

I see both the terms, "can" and "will" as attitudes. But I see "will" as applying a little extra effort. I already know you "can" do anything, but "will" you do it? In life we face adversity and opposition and at other times we face no resistance at all, but the "will" of someone can take them through it all. I have never heard a coach say in sports, when you have an opponent to their breaking point, "Let's break their can." A coach typically says, "Let's break their will."

Task: Find the "will" within you. Stop selling yourself and others short with "I can" statements. Rather, begin saying, "I will." This does not mean that you have to say "yes" to everything. Be cautious. Use common sense but make the effort and see what happens in your life and the lives around you.

Day 20: Practice

"Practice makes perfect, but nobody is perfect, so why do we have to practice?" –Quote from a friend

Growing up, my friends and I adopted the above quote. For the longest time, we were always told that practice makes perfect. While the saying made sense as teens, we rationalized that no one was perfect; therefore, practice did not really matter.

I can still recall as a freshman in high school when I learned what the term practice really meant. Being a freshman typically meant you were seldom used on the varsity team. So I made a decision, and I skipped my first football practice. I skipped so I could go and play basketball with all of my older friends. It was a beautiful fall day, and there were about ten or so of us on the blacktop court, playing our hearts out. As we continued to play, I watched as my dad passed by and stopped at the local gas station. My heart sunk, I noticed him, and I was sure he noticed me, but I hoped that he didn't. As I got home that evening, he pulled me aside and asked me if I was playing. I answered "yes", there was no need to lie about it, he already knew. Then he said, "You need to make a decision. Are you going to be a football player, or are you going to be on the team? If it is more important to play basketball with friends, then you need to go to the coach and tell him. However, if you are going to be a football player you need to become the best teammate and dedicate yourself to them, as your time will come."

From that moment on, I never missed another football practice. It didn't matter if I was injured or sick. I showed up and supported my team.

I have never heard anyone say they really enjoy practice. Just a little over 10 years ago, a basketball player by the name of Allen Iverson went into an interview to address practice. He probably delivered one of the most unique, bizarre individual rants on practice ever. Iverson used the word roughly 20 times in his rant. His overall theme was that "why are we talking about practice, I go out every day and perform and play in those games. I am one of the greatest players of my time, and we are in here talking about practice."

Philippians 4:9 says "Whatever you have learned or received or heard from me, or seen in me – put into practice. And the God of Peace will be with you."

It is simple. Practice might not bring us to perfection. The goal of life is not to become perfect, however. Let's face it, we will never be perfect. Practice should be viewed as maturity and growth, not perfection. By practicing we learn a lot about ourselves. We learn how to deal with situations and practice to become a better person inwardly and outwardly. Practice is not simple or easy. In fact, it is hard work, which is why they call it practice. While practice is difficult, it will take us a long way into becoming perfect.

Task: Forget about the word perfect as we will never be perfect. Starting looking at perfect from a growth and maturing perspective as Paul wrote about in Philippians. Think of how you can use the quote "Practice makes perfect" (growth and maturing) in your daily life. Continue to practice what is good and right and everything else will fall into place.

Day 21: Rest

Instead of giving you encouraging words about pressing onward through week three, I give you The Carpenter's Story. What a great read about one's effort and attitude.

The Carpenter's Story

Author Unknown

An elderly carpenter was ready to retire. He told his employer-contractor of his plans to leave the house building business and live a more leisurely life with his wife and enjoying his extended family.

He would miss the paycheck, but he needed to retire. They could get by. The contractor was sorry to see his good worker go and asked if he could build just one more house as a personal favor. The carpenter said yes, but in time it was easy to see that his heart was not in his work. He resorted to shoddy workmanship and used inferior materials. It was an unfortunate way to end his career.

When the carpenter finished his work and the builder came to inspect the house, the contractor handed the front-door key to the carpenter. "This is your house," he said, "my gift to you."
What a shock! What a shame!

If he had only known he was building his own house, he would have done it all so differently. Now he had to live in the home he had built none too well.

So it is with us. We build our lives in a distracted way, reacting rather than acting and being willing to give our best. At important points, we do not give the job our best effort. Then with a shock we look at the situation we have created and find that we are now living in the house we have built. If we had realized that, we would have done it differently.

Think of yourself as the carpenter. Think about your house. Each day you hammer a nail, place a board, or erect a wall. Build wisely. It is the only life you will ever build. Even if you live it for only one day more, that day deserves to be lived graciously and with dignity. The plaque on the wall says, "Life is a do-it-yourself project."

Your life tomorrow will be the result of your attitudes and the choices you make today.

The Man Who Thinks He Can

By Walter D. Wintle

If you think you are beaten, you are;
If you think you dare not, you don't.
If you'd like to win, but think you can't,
It's almost a cinch you won't.

If you think you'll lose, you're lost,
For out in the world we find
Success begins with a fellow's will;
It's all in the state of mind.

If you think you're outclassed, you are;
You've got to think high to rise.
You've got to be sure of yourself before
You can ever win a prize.

Life's battles don't always go
To the stronger or faster man;
But soon or late the man who wins
Is the one who thinks he can.

Chapter 4

Dreams

Day 22: Dreams

"Be a dreamer. If you don't know how to dream, you're dead."
Jim Valvano

Dreams are simply defined as a strongly desired goal or purpose (Merriam-Webster Dictionary). Although there are numerous definitions of dreams, I want to focus on the dreams that each of us have – the ones that drive us and not some unconscious story we conjure up while in a sleeping state. As children, some of us dream of being teachers, doctors, lawyers and the list goes on. As a child, I wanted to be an airplane pilot as a result of watching the movie, Top Gun. Later, I wanted to pursue a career as a professional football player and next a history teacher and then a banker. Dreams are what motivate us and keep us striving for potentially unreachable realities. Some of us will obtain our dreams and some of us will only be left with unfulfilled dreams.. My goal is for you to not only dream, but rather to dream big. As the late Hall of Famer and North Carolina State Basketball Coach Jim Valvano said, "Be a dreamer. If you don't know how to dream, you're dead." This statement rings true.

Many of the greatest success stories throughout history began with a dream. In 1963, Dr. Martin Luther King Jr. delivered, in my opinion, one of the most moving speeches ever. King Jr's "I Have a Dream" speech brought about positivity at a time when there was so much negativity surrounding civil rights. Following is an excerpt from his speech,

"I say to you today, my friends, so even though we face the difficulties of today and tomorrow, I still have a dream. It is a dream deeply rooted in the American dream."

I will be honest. I am a dreamer. I am a dreamer in the truest extent of the word. I am always caught up in bigger goals and ideas. Some of my ideas are realistic, and some maybe not so achievable. Regardless, I still dream. Sometimes my dreams have gotten in the way of life's reality. Yet I still dream. See, I believe that if we set our minds to something then we can achieve just about anything. The only thing that can really stop us is ourselves. Have you ever thought that you had the greatest idea in the world only to have someone step all over that idea and tell you that it was unobtainable or unreachable? Maybe others have told you to stop dreaming.

As I set out on the quest of writing a book (my dream). I was told that I lacked the dedication, that I never committed to anything, and that I start out strong and fade within time. As I started writing this book, the dream transformed into reality. I had something that could be seen and read. Then as I became more confident, and more comfortable, I allowed people to read samplings of my book. Receiving feedback, both positive and negative, made the dream became more realistic. People started to realize that I meant business, and I was not playing. More importantly, I realized that my dream was alive.

As you read the book, you probably have realized that I am a very optimistic person. I have learned that being positive and optimistic is not a characteristic people always enjoy. We have been conditioned around negativity and pessimistic perspectives. If you do not believe me, watch the weather or the evening news. Everything is usually delivered from a negative outlook. However, much like the weather and news, the influencers in our lives, are much the same. I paint a positive picture, because I believe in dreams and what dreams mean to us. I believe that within each of us lies a dreamer that has fully untapped potential. I also believe that first we have to believe in ourselves. Believing in ourselves leads to believing in our dreams, and when we believe in our dream, we can then make our dreams a reality.

Task: I challenge you as an individual to dream big. If you already dream big, I challenge you to dream even bigger. Our minds are powerful. Within ourselves lies untapped potential, potential only we know the limits of. Stop worrying about what people say or think. Influencers have held you hostage long enough. Realize that you are in control of you. I have always been told that if I dream it and believe it, then I can do it. You can too. Adopt that mindset and see where this life can and will take you.

Day 23: Goals

"A goal is a dream set to paper. Don't just think it—ink it."

Author Unknown

At my new employee orientation, I was given a book written by Dan Zadra, entitled *5: Where will you be five years from today?* It was this book that I give credit to sparking my goal to write this book and start my company. Within the pages laid so many thought provoking quotes and stories that caused a stirring within me. I believe that it is great to have dreams, but to have goals is even better. Take a moment, grab a pen, paper, and write down your goals. By articulating your dreams, you are more likely to reach the goals you set for yourself.

We all have goals. Our goals range in size. Some are small and some are large. Some are obtainable, and some not so easily obtained. The key component that drives a goal to success or failure lies within you. We are the master craftsman, orchestrator, and leader of our paths and futures. What is more important though, is that we also have someone on our team who can help us as we move along life's path and work towards meeting these goals. We have to realize that we are not alone in the progression.

As I started looking to create my company, I sought lots of input from others who had started companies. For the most part, each of them told me that it started with a dream and goals for their visions. I was told of the many negatives that come with writing a book and going into the speaking industry. I was reminded that the journey is not easy. It is a lot of hard work. It was not until I met with a man whom I have much appreciation for and admire for his work, that I understood the whole concept of obtaining one's goals.

On a wet, gloomy day, I met with Coach D Robinson in Lexington, KY to discuss with him my plans. I had known Coach D for many years, and our paths had crossed several times since I started recruiting in education. I met him for the first time at a college fair on the campus of Berea College. There was no easy way a person could miss him. People were drawn to him by his physical stature and appearance and if that was not enough his commanding voice filled the room. As I got to know him, I found there was more to him, and I think his compassion and willingness to assist people is what hooked me. However, as I met with him on that day, I realized that no dream, goal, or pursuit can truly be completed until we allow God the opportunity to bless us and our decision. Coach D told me "that there are tons of successful people in the speaking world, but place God in control of it all, and no matter how much negativity surrounded me, it would all work out the way its suppose to." Who knew a simple day in Lexington, KY at Panera Bread with a person that I have the utmost respect for, was all that I needed to inspire my dreams and turn them into goals.

As months have passed I realize that goals, especially big ones, take a lot of energy, prayer and sacrifice, but when the dream/goals starts to take form and reality sets in, the work and time, is well worth it. My advice to anyone who has dreams and goals is to never back down, never stop striving to make them a true reality. The only person that can hold you back is you and you alone. There are struggles and issues that will arise along the way and when you feel that there is no hope, no end ahead, turn it over to God and He will assist you along the way.

Verse: Philippians 3:13-14: Brothers, I do not consider that I have made it my own. But one thing I do: forgetting what lies behind and straining forward to what lies ahead, I press on toward the goal for the prize of the upward call of God in Christ Jesus.

Task: Get to work on your dreams and goals. Write down all of the things you want to achieve no matter how big or small. It you can think it, you can do it. Remember when you feel that you are becoming weighed down and you can no longer press onward to obtain your goals, give it over to God and He will see you through.

Day 24: Never Quit

"Don't give up. Don't ever give up." - Jim Valvano

Approximately two years ago, I started to write this book. I have had numerous excuses and road blocks along the way that have derailed its completion. However, I never lost sight, never once forgot about the dream of penning my own book. I have sat down in front of the computer over a thousand hours in the past two years, doing homework, completing work related documents, surfing the Internet and staring at a screen that basically intimidated me. Somewhere, however, I found a renewed spirit to finally start again and eventually finish. It is only fitting that I do so, as I constantly preach to students daily "It is not where you start that matters. It is where you finish." These words, that in the past I only used to motivate people, have become my purpose.

In life, it is so easy to start something only to never see the completion. We blame time, circumstances or anything for our failed attempts instead of taking on personal responsibility. Coach Valvano's words pierce the soul. As he was battling cancer, he said his famous words, "Don't give up, Don't ever give up." If you can read those words and not be inspired, I am not sure what else will.

Think about this. We start a task or hobby, and we are overly excited about it. We will sink every ounce of our being into our new experiences only to slowly let it fade away into a passing thought. Why do we do this? Mainly because we lose interest. We lose that drive that we once had. We lose the excitement. All the positives that once surrounded us fade, and we lose sight of why we ever started our task or hobby to begin with it. It is not that we cannot complete the task or master our hobbies, but other things take our attention away from the things that we started. Emotions get in the way, and we start to question ourselves and intentions. Slowly we give way to the negativity that is usually self-inflicted. We have to learn to defeat that negativity, change our mindsets, and finish what we start.

When we get to the point of quitting, we need to stop and reassess why we ever started to begin with. As the saying goes, "When we get knocked down, get up, dust off and start again." That is the mindset that we need to have. The good news is, we can do it if we just get the mindset right. As a teenager I remember posters in school that encouraged us to "Do our best", to "Try hard", "If we fail to try, try, try again." It is the little things from our past, present and future that will assist us in moving forward, to not give up and to press onward.

Task: Today find that renewed spirit and energy of why you started that hobby or task in the first place. Dust it off, unpack it from a hidden place, and slowly start back to finishing what you started. When you start to falter or lose sight again, remember Matthew 19:26 "With God, All things are possible."

Day 25: Discouraged to Encouraged

"This is the beginning of a new day. You have been given this day to use as you will. You can waste it or use it for good. What you do today is important because you are exchanging a day of your life for it. When tomorrow comes, this day will be gone forever; in its place is something that you have left behind...let it be something good."

Author Unknown

In this day and age it is so easy to become discouraged. There are many reasons that we become discouraged. There are events that take place in our lives that will leave us sad, bitter, overwhelmed or discouraged. We study hard only to receive a grade that is less than we anticipated. We do not get the job that we had hoped for. We receive bad news about a friend or family member. Our efforts do not meet our expectations. Our effort then impacts our attitude. Then effort and attitude hinder our dreams. When things do not go the way we expect, we typically ask "Why me?" I say, "Why not me." We must be reminded daily there is a reason to everything. Maybe these little hiccups are blessings in disguise. Maybe God is testing us in small doses. Many times, what seems like a large disappointment is nothing more than a minor detour. What we must do is change our way of thinking. We must reverse our negative thoughts and create positive thoughts that will wash away discouragement and bring about encouragement. As they say, "it is always darkest before the dawn."

81

Discouragement is the lack of courage or confidence. There are many things that cause discouragement. The cause of our discouragement can come in many areas; emotional, physical, spiritual challenges or a combination of all. Being discouraged makes every situation that we face seem impossible. The good news is that we can overcome all of our discouragements because of God. There is nothing that He cannot overcome. No matter how big or small our current situation, our God can and will overcome.

We can overcome our discouraging moments with known Biblical encouragement. Isaiah 41:10, for example, tells us, "Fear not, for I am with you…" Knowing that should be more than enough assurance and bring all the encouragement that we need to make it through anything we may face. These little stumbling/roadblocks are merely that. These are test that each of us must face. These tests are designed, created to test our faith, our endurance, and our will. Sure we may hit the bottom of the ocean floor before we find our footing. However, when we find our footing we have choices. Sink, stay down and never resurface, or find our footing, look up and push off that floor, and break the surface to a new beginning.

In life we have to make choices. We can be happy or sad, mad or glad. We can choose to take a new path or continue on the path we are on. The good news is that we can find encouragement in our discouragement, because God is with us, and if God is with us, who or what can be against us?

Task: What has discouraged you over the course of the last few weeks, months and years? Are you ready to take your new found encouragement and defeat what has discouraged you? Write down all the things you have felt discouraged about and seek out ways to bring about change with your new found encouragement

Day 26: Motivated

"You ain't gonna believe this, but you used to fit right here. (He gestures to the palm of his hand). I'd hold you up to say to your mother, 'This kid's gonna be the best kid in the world. This kid's gonna be somebody better than anybody I ever knew.' And you grew up good and wonderful. It was great just watchin' you, every day was like a privilege. Then the time came for you to be your own man and take on the world, and you did. But somewhere along the line, you changed. You stopped being you. You let people stick a finger in your face and tell you you're no good. And when things got hard, you started lookin' for something to blame, like a big shadow.

Let me tell you something you already know. The world ain't all sunshine and rainbows. It's a very mean and nasty place, and I don't care how tough you are, it will beat you to your knees and keep you there permanently if you let it. You, me, or nobody is gonna hit as hard as life. But it ain't about how hard you hit, it's about how hard you can get hit and keep moving forward. How much you can take and keep moving forward. That's how winning is done!

Now if you know what you're worth, then go out and get what you're worth! But you gotta be willing to take the hits. And not pointing fingers saying you ain't where you wanna be because of him, or her, or anybody! Cowards do that and that ain't you! You're better than that!

I'm always gonna love you no matter what. No matter what happens. You're my son and you're my blood. You're the best thing in my life. But until you start believing in yourself, you ain't gonna have a life." – Rocky Balboa

The above scene in the movie Rocky Balboa, it is a real turning point to such a great series. Rocky was always the underdog but was always determined to prove people wrong and change their perspective of this man. Merriam-Webster Dictionary defines motivation as the act or process of motivating, the condition of being motivated. I believe motivation is something we must find within ourselves. We can seek it from others, or we can try to use accomplishments and accolades. Yet, until we find it within ourselves, it is worthless. We can find motivation from a lot of places. We can find it from people who lead, we can read books about it or we can accomplish something great. However, in the end, we have to believe that we are great.

Search the Internet about motivation. You may be surprised at all the information you will find about the subject. There are numerous results that will be shown from authors, to published books, videos, pictures, and quotes. It is great to see all of that information. We can read it, watch it, print it and put it in a place that we constantly frequent. We have to choose to be motivated. We have to make a decision to enhance our efforts, giving more of ourselves. We have to change our attitudes, becoming more positive, believing we can achieve anything and nothing can or will stop us from reaching our goals and seeing our dreams become a reality.

Matthew 19:26 tells us, But Jesus looked at them and said, "With man this is impossible, but with God all things are possible." What more motivation do you need? When we get to the point that we feel we can no longer push onward, we feel that our efforts are worthless, that there is no way our hopes and dreams can become a reality. Remember with God all things are possible. Sometimes in life, we have to surrender ourselves to God and receive our motivation from divine circumstances.

Task: What motivates you? What is that driving force in your life? Got it? Harness it. Use it to achieve all this world has for you. No one, I mean no one can defeat you but yourself.

Day 27: Empowered

"Don't ask yourself what the world needs; ask yourself what
makes you come alive. And then go and do that. Because what
the world needs are people who have come alive."

- Dr. Howard Thurman

Imagine that today you woke up, and you were empowered
with all the knowledge and wisdom known to man-kind, which
would be an abundant supply of fortune. What would you do with it?
Would you create the next social media site? Would you work
tirelessly to find a cure for cancer or the common cold, or would you
choose to do nothing?

The truth is that we all have abilities, talents, and purposes
within each of us. Unfortunately we are sometimes so blinded by the
other things in the world that we cannot recognize them. Here is
something I want to share with you. This might be the most powerful
thing that you will ever be told "God made you." Genesis 2:7 says,
"Then the Lord God formed the man of dust from the ground and
breathed into his nostrils the breath of life, and the man became a
living creature." God made us in His own perfect image. He knew
us before we were born. He laid a foundation of greatness before us.
It is so great. We will take the rest of our lives trying to unveil all
there is to this greatness. God gave us a purpose. He has given us
talents. It is our choice to use them accordingly. God has
empowered us with the ability to choose how we would like to use

these gifts. We can use them for the greater good, we can keep them hidden, or we can do nothing.

Within each of us lie talents that we may recognize immediately or talents that may lie dormant for years before we realize what we are truly good at and what our purpose truly is. It took me a lot of time, a lot of indecision, and lots of disappointments to come to the realization of what my purpose and talents were. I was lost. However, when I finally fully surrendered myself to God, I began to recognize my path. Once I found it, I have never once questioned where I am today. My talents have led me to where I am today. It led me to work for a company where I could hone my public speaking skills, start a company, write a book and assist in shaping the future generations. When I first started my career, I passed on my knowledge of educational opportunities to students. As the years have passed, I now motivate and empower kids, not only on educational opportunities, but also to motivate and empower them about themselves, their abilities and to explore their talents.

Here is the truth, I cannot wave a magical wand and show you the answers to all of life's multiple questions. I wish I could, but I am not that powerful. I lack that skill set. What I can do though is tell you these things: Life is not easy. There are no shortcuts to get where you want to be. You will have to deal with trials. You will have to deal with disappointments, failures and mistakes. You will get mad, feel hurt, and experience sadness and loss. You will face jealousy, maybe become resentful. But, I can also tell you this. You are loved. You are special. You have more greatness than you will ever know. You are powerful. You cannot be held back by anyone but yourself. You have the ability to become whatever you want to be with hard work and dedication. You were made in God's image and nothing else is more important than knowing that.

I leave you with this. The most powerful and insightful final thought I can give you. Over 2,000 years ago, God decided to become flesh in the form of Jesus. He came to the Earth to dwell amongst man-kind. He dwelt among sinners and saints. He came for one reason alone. He was mocked and persecuted, beaten and bruised, spit upon and put to death upon a cross to die for all man's sins. Not because He had too, but rather because He loves us that much. He wants us to live with Him eternally. Why? Because, HE LOVES YOU AND ME.

John 3:16 says, "For God so loved the world, that he gave his only Son, that whoever believes in him should not perish but have eternal life."

Task: Reflect on the past 27 days of this devotional. Have you experienced transformation? Do you look at life any differently? Write down how your life has changed, how you want to change in the future. Write down your goals and dreams and follow through on them.

Day 28: Rest

"It is finished" John 19:30

Congratulations!!! I bet you thought you might never make it to this day. I know it probably has not been easy. For me, writing the book was not easy, but God assisted me through to the end. Today marks the end of a 28 day devotional journey. I hope you are better today than you were when you began your journey. I am proud of you and your commitment. Maybe you took a few extra days to finish. Guess what though. You stuck with it and finished it. It is easy to say "Mission accomplished" and forget about what the past 28 days has meant. This devotional also can be used to address many issues in your life at certain points. Pick it back up and reread it one day if need be, pass it on to someone else, or use it as reference from time to time. I thank you for taking the time to devote necessary to this journey.

Being the last day, I hope that you have renewed your spirit, rekindled a flame that has flickered to just a warm ember. Maybe you can bring about change in your life that will be everlasting for generations to come.

My prayer is that you can take the words (not my words, but words given by God) and reflect upon the experiences and transform your life, even if only minimally. My God-given purpose has been to help you realize that you can leverage any situation you are in, applying some effort, transforming your attitudes to realize your dreams. That is the purpose of L.E.A.D.

I also pray that if you have not found Christ, that today, you will do that? If you are a Christian, I pray that your walk is renewed and that you can become the salt and light of the world God wants you to be.

Isaiah 40:31 says, "But they who wait for the Lord shall renew their strength; they shall mount up with wings like eagles; they shall run and not be weary; they shall walk and not faint."

Matthew 25:21 says, "His master replied, 'Well done, good and faithful servant! You have been faithful with a few things; I will put you in charge of many things. Come and share your master's happiness!'

SERENITY PRAYER
REINHOLD NIEBUHR

GOD GRANT ME THE SERENITY
TO ACCEPT THE THINGS I CANNOT CHANGE;
COURAGE TO CHANGE THE THINGS I CAN;
AND WISDOM TO KNOW THE DIFFERENCE.

LIVING ONE DAY AT A TIME;
ENJOYING ONE MOMENT AT A TIME;
ACCEPTING HARDSHIPS AS THE PATHWAY TO PEACE;
TAKING, AS HE DID, THIS SINFUL WORLD
AS IT IS, NOT AS I WOULD HAVE IT;
TRUSTING THAT HE WILL MAKE ALL THINGS RIGHT
IF I SURRENDER TO HIS WILL;
THAT I MAY BE REASONABLY HAPPY IN THIS LIFE
AND SUPREMELY HAPPY WITH HIM
FOREVER IN THE NEXT.
AMEN.

(ONE OF MY MOTHER'S FAVORITES)

Chapter 5

Spiritual Assistance

Are you ready to commit your life but do not know how follow these simple steps via The ABCs of Becoming a Christian:

"A" is for Admit. You must admit to God that you are a sinner.

- Romans 3:23 For all have sinned and fall short of the glory of God,.
- Romans 6:23 For the wages of sin is death, but the gift of God is eternal life in Christ Jesus our Lord.
- Acts 3:19 Repent, then, and turn to God, so that your sins may be wiped out, that times of refreshing may come from the Lord,
- 1 John 1:9 If we confess our sins, He is faithful and just and will forgive us our sins and purify us from all unrighteousness.

"B" is for Believe. You must believe that Jesus is God's Son and that God sent Jesus to pay the penalty for sin.

- John 3:16 For God so loved the world that He gave His one and only Son, that whoever believes in Him shall not perish but have eternal life.

- John 14:6 Jesus answered, "I am the way and the truth and the life. No one comes to the Father except through me."

- Romans 5:8 But God demonstrates His own love for us in this: While we were still sinners, Christ died for us.

"C" is for Confess. You must confess your faith in Jesus Christ as Savior and Lord.

- Romans 10:9-10, 13 That if you confess with your mouth, "Jesus is Lord," and believe in your heart that God raised Him from the dead, you will be saved. For it is with your heart that you believe and are justified, and it is with your mouth that you confess and are saved…. for, "Everyone who calls on the name of the Lord will be saved."

Sinners Prayer

Dear God,

I know that I am a sinner, and that I need Your grace. Thank you for loving me enough to send your Son Jesus Christ into the world to die for my sins. I believe that He arose from the dead and that He lives today. I confess my sins to You now, and ask that You place Your Holy Spirit in my heart that I may turn away from my sins. I love You, I believe in You, and I want to have a personal relationship with You.

In Jesus' name I pray, Amen.

Use Your Fingers When You Pray

1. Thumb (people who are close to you)
Your thumb is nearest to you. So begin your prayers by praying for those closest to you. They are the easiest to remember. To pray for our loved ones is, as C.S. Lewis once said, a "sweet duty".

2. Pointer (people who point the way)
The next finger is the pointing finger. Pray for those who teach, instruct and heal. This includes teachers, doctors, and ministers. They need support and wisdom in pointing others in the right direction. Keep them in your prayers.

3. Tall Finger (people in authority)
The next finger is the tallest finger. It reminds us of our leaders. Pray for the president, leaders in business and industry, and administrators. These people shape our nation and guide public opinion. They need God's guidance.

4. Ring Finger (people who are weak)
The fourth finger is our ring finger. Surprising to many is the fact that this is our weakest finger; as any piano teacher will testify. It should remind us to pray for those who are weak, in trouble or in pain. They need your prayers day and night. You cannot pray too much for them.

5. Little Finger (your own needs)
Lastly, comes our little finger; the smallest finger of all. Which is where we should place ourselves in relation to God and others. As the Bible says, "the least shall be the greatest among you." Your pinky should remind you to pray for yourself. By the time you have prayed for the other four groups, your own needs will be put into proper perspective and you will be able to pray for yourself more effectively.

Random Quotes and Stories

Additional Motivational Quotes

"Our greatest glory is not in never failing, but in rising up every time we fail." - Ralph Waldo Emerson

"The growth and development of people is the highest calling of leadership." -Harvey S. Firestone

"The final test of a leader is that he [she] leaves behind in others the conviction and will to carry on." -Walter Lippman

"If we all did the things we are really capable of doing, we would literally astound ourselves." -Thomas Edison

"I can choose to let it define me, confine me, refine me, outshine me or I can choose to move on and leave it behind me." - Author Unknown

"To the question of your life, you are the only answer. To the problems of your life, you are the only solution." - Jo Coudert, *Advice From A Failure*

"Out of all the things that I have achieved, one of the things that I have learned, is it's not necessarily what you have achieved in life that matters most, but it's who you become in the process of those achievements that really matters." – Curtis Martin

ATTITUDE IS EVERYTHING

Jerry was the kind of guy you love to hate. He was always in a good mood and always had something positive to say. When someone would ask him how he was doing, he would reply, "If I were any better, I would be twins!"

He was a unique manager because he had several waiters who had followed him around from restaurant to restaurant. The reason the waiters followed Jerry was because of his attitude. He was a natural motivator. If an employee was having a bad day, Jerry was there telling the employee how to look on the positive side of the situation.

Seeing this style really made me curious, so one day I went up to Jerry and asked him, "I don't get it! You can't be a positive person all of the time. How do you do it?"

Jerry replied, "Each morning I wake up and say to myself, Jerry, you have two choices today. You can choose to be in a good mood or you can choose to be in a bad mood.' I choose to be in a good mood. Each time something bad happens, I can choose to be a victim or I can choose to learn from it. I choose to learn from it. Every time someone comes to me complaining, I can choose to accept their complaining or I can point out the positive side of life. I choose the positive side of life."

"Yeah, right, it's not that easy", I protested.

"Yes it is," Jerry said. "Life is all about choices. When you cut away all the junk, every situation is a choice. You choose how you react to situations. You choose how people will affect your mood. You choose to be in a good mood or bad mood. The bottom line: It's your choice how you live life."

I reflected on what Jerry said. Soon thereafter, I left the restaurant industry to start my own business. We lost touch, but often thought about him when I made a choice about life instead of reacting to it.

Several years later, I heard that Jerry did something you are never supposed to do in a restaurant business: he left the back door open one morning, and was held up at gunpoint by three armed robbers. While trying to open the safe, his hand, shaking from nervousness, slipped off the combination. The robbers panicked and shot him. Luckily, Jerry was found relatively quickly and rushed to the local trauma center.

After 18 hours of surgery and weeks of intensive care, Jerry was released from the hospital with fragments of the bullets still in his body. I saw Jerry about six months after the accident. When I asked him how he was, he replied, "If I were any better, I'd be twins. Wanna see my scars?"

I declined to see his wounds, but did ask him what had gone through his mind as the robbery took place. "The first thing that went through my mind was that I should have locked the back door", Jerry replied.

"Then, as I lay on the floor, I remembered that I had two choices: I could choose to live, or I could choose to die. I chose to live.

"Weren't you scared? Did you lose consciousness?", I asked.

Jerry continued, "The paramedics were great. They kept telling me I was going to be fine. But when they wheeled me into the emergency room and I saw the expressions on the faces of the doctors and nurses, I got really scared. In their eyes, I read, 'He's a dead man'. I knew I needed to take action."

"What did you do?" I asked.

"Well, there was a big, burly nurse shouting questions at me", said Jerry. She asked if I was allergic to anything. "Yes", I replied. The doctors and nurses stopped working as they waited for my reply... I took a deep breath and yelled, "Bullets!" Over their laughter, I told them, "I am choosing to live. Operate on me as if I am alive, not dead."

Jerry lived, thanks to the skill of his doctors, but also because of his amazing attitude. I learned from him that every day we have the choice to live fully. Attitude, after all, is everything.

Discouragement - A Tool of the Devil

Once upon a time, it was announced that the devil was going out of business and would sell all his equipment to those who were willing to pay the price.

On the big day of the sale, all his tools were attractively displayed. There were Envy, Jealousy, Hatred, Malice, Deceit, Sensuality, Pride, Idolatry, and other implements of evil display. Each of the tools was marked with its own price tag.

Over in the corner by itself was a harmless-looking, wedge-shaped tool that looked very much worn, but still it bore a higher price tag than any of the other tools. Someone asked the devil what it was, and he answered, "That is Discouragement."

The next question came quickly, "And why is this tool priced so high even though it is plain to see that it is more worn than the others?"

"Because," replied the devil, "This tool is more useful to me than all the other tools. I can pry open and get into any person's heart with this tool when I cannot get near the person with any other tool. Once I find my way inside the

101

human heart, I can manipulate the person that I am attacking in whatever way suits me best. I have used this wonderful tool to my best advantage by sending people to their graves earlier through suicide, by turning the hearts of people away from God and away from His salvation plan through Jesus Christ, by shaking, destroying and ruining the faith of every Christian around the globe, by setting off an amazing domino effect of discouragement and discord in so many churches and their ministries, and by causing all backsliders and prodigals to believe that there is no hope in life so that they may remain utterly lost in their sinful state. Discouragement is a tool which is so worn because I have used it destructively on everybody in the world, and very, very few people even realize that this tool belongs to me."

This tool was priced so high that no one could buy it, and to this very day it has never been sold. It still belongs to the devil, and he still uses it on mankind.

Beware the wiles of the evil one who seeks to destroy our lives through his ever wicked tool of Discouragement..

~ Author Unknown

Footprints in the Sand

By Mary Stevenson

One night I dreamed I was walking along the beach with the Lord. Many scenes from my life flashed across the sky. In each scene I noticed footprints in the sand. Sometimes there were two sets of footprints, other times there were one set of footprints.

This bothered me because I noticed that during the low periods of my life, when I was suffering from anguish, sorrow or defeat, I could see only one set of footprints.

So I said to the Lord, "You promised me Lord, that if I followed you, you would walk with me always. But I have noticed that during the most trying periods of my life there have only been one set of footprints in the sand. Why, when I needed you most you have not been there for me?"

The Lord replied, "The times when you have seen only one set of footprints, is when I carried you."

Hand in Hand

By Joyce Smith

Together, the road of life we'll walk

There will be joy and laughter, tears and sadness,

Grief and sorrow,

But we will be Hand in Hand

The days will seem dreary and cold,

The nights long and dark,

Shadows around us will fall,

The burdens will seem too much to bear

But with love we can make it

Hand in Hand

The road may be long and narrow,

The hills too high to climb

The valleys will be wide and the waters deep

But we will be Hand in Hand

When our trials are over and beauty around us flow

When our dreams come true,

And we reach the other shore,

We will always walk Hand in Hand

References

Attitude. (n.d). Merriam-Webster Online. Retrieved from
  http://www.merriam-webster.com/dictionary/attitude

Attitude Story. Retrieved from
  http://www.agiftofinspiration.com.au/stories/attitude/Attitude.shtm
  l

Challenges Quotes. Retrieved from
  http://www.finestquotes.com/select_quote-category-Challenges-
  page-0.htm#ixzz1zesI9A3t

Coelho, Paulo http://www.spiritual-short-stories.com/spiritual-short-story-
  315-Overcoming+Obstacles.html

Coudert, J., *Advice From A Failure.* Retrieved from
  http://www.quotegarden.com/be-great.html

Daph. (2006). Discouragement..a Tool of the Devil. Retrieved from
  http://lifeternity.blogspot.com/2006/07/discouragementa-tool-of-
  devil.html

Devers, G. Quote. Retrieved from
  http://www.brainyquote.com/quotes/quotes/g/gaildevers144884.ht
  ml

Dreams. (n.d.). Merriam Webster Online. Retrieved from
  http://www.merriam-webster.com/dictionary/dreams

Edison, T. Quote. Retrieved from
  http://www.thomasedison.com/quotes.html

Effort. (n.d.). Merriam Webster Online. Retrieved from
  http://www.merriam-webster.com/dictionary/effort

Emerson, Ralph W. Quotes. Retrieved from
  http://www.heartsandminds.org/quotes/effort.htm

  http://www.livelifehappy.com/i-can-choose-to-let-it-define-me-
  confine-me-refine-me-outshine-me/

Firestone, H. S. Quote. Retrieved from
    http://www.brainyquote.com/quotes/authors/h/harvey_s_firestone.
    html

Gafka, M. Quote. Retrieve from
    http://picturethatquote.blogspot.com/2011/04/to-be-successful-
    you-must-accept-all.html

Helen Keller. Retrieved from http://www.biography.com/people/helen-
    keller-9361967

Hill, Napoleon
    http://www.brainyquote.com/quotes/keywords/influence.html#ciY
    e0LpkRHQ1AVw7.99

Horace. Quote. Retrieved from
    http://www.studymode.com/essays/Adversity-Has-The-Effect-Of-
    Eliciting-1551049.html

Iverson, Allen quote
    http://sportsillustrated.cnn.com/basketball/news/2002/05/09/iverso
    n_transcript/

Jefferson, T. Quote. Retrieved from
    http://www.monticello.org/site/jefferson/nothing-can-stop-man-
    right-mental-attitude-quotation

Jordan, M. Quotes. Retrieved from
    http://www.brainyquote.com/search_results.html?q=michael+jorda
    n

Kaggwa, S. Retrieved from http://thinkexist.com/quotation/try_and_fail-
    but_don-t_fail_to_try/220298.html

King Jr, Dr. Martin Luther, "I Have A Dream". Washington. 28 Aug.
    1963.
Kissinger, H. Quote. Retrieved from
    http://www.brainyquote.com/quotes/quotes/h/henryakis130663.ht
    ml

Kohl, D. (2012). Quote. A Lifetime of Wisdon.com. Retrieved from
    http://alifetimeofwisdom.com/success/what-dream/

Leadership. (n.d.). Merriam-Webster Online. Retrieved from http://www.merriam-webster.com/dictionary/leadership

Lippman, W. Quote. Retrieved from http://www.great-quotes.com/leadership_quotes.htm

Lombardi, V. Quote. Retrieved from http://www.vincelombardi.com/quotes.html

Martin, C. Retrieved from http://www.bing.com/videos/search?q=curtis+martin+hall+of+fame+speech&mid=98C0BE9BDF16F1DF53D098C0BE9BDF16F1DF53D0&view=detail&FORM=VIRE1 Retrieved on Aug 15, 2012

McKinney, M. (2010). lead:ology-What is Leadership? Leadershipnow.com. Retrieved from http://www.leadershipnow.com/leadingblog/2010/05/leadology_what_is_leadership.html

Niebuhr, R. (n.d.). Serenity Prayer. Retrieved from ttp://www.beliefnet.com/Prayers/Protestant/Addiction/Serenity-Prayer.aspx#M9ZdD1dVhkcwO7LY.99

Oprah Winfrey. Retrieved from http://www.achievement.org/autodoc/page/win0bio-1

Peck, M.S. Quote. Retrieved from http://www.goodreads.com/quotes/52532-the-truth-is-that-our-finest-moments-are-most-likely

Powell, C. Quote. Retrieved from http://www.brainyquote.com/quotes/quotes/c/colinpowel144992.html

Radwan, M.F. *Believe in Yourself and People Will Be Forced to Believe in You.* Retrieved from http://www.2knowmyself.com/Success/Believe_in_yourself

Riggio, R.E. (2009, March 18). *Leaders: Born or Made?.* Cutting-Edge Leadership. Retrieved from http://www.psychologytoday.com/blog/cutting-edge-leadership/200903/leaders-born-or-made

Riley, P. Quote. Retrieved from
    http://thinkexist.com/quotation/if_you_have_a_positive_attitude_a
    nd_constantly/256632.html

Rocky's Inspirations Speech to His Son. Retrieved from
    http://www.goodsirs.net/warrior/rockys-inspirational-speech-to-
    his-son/

Rohn, J. Quote. Retrieved from
    http://thinkexist.com/quotation/leadership_is_the_challenge_to_be
    _something_more/261572.html

Scrapbook.com. Quote. Retrieved from
    http://www.scrapbook.com/quotes/doc/7518.html

Smith, J. (n.d.) Hand in Hand Poem.

Stevenson, M. Footprints in the Sand. Retrieved from
    http://www.footprints-inthe-
    sand.com/index.php?page=Poem/Poem.php

Swindoll, C. Quote. Retrieved from
    http://www.goodreads.com/author/quotes/5139.Charles_R_Swindo
    ll

Thatcher, M. Quote. Retrieved from
    http://www.quoteauthors.com/quotes/margaret-thatcher-
    quotes.html

The ABCs of Becoming a Christian. Retrieved from
    http://www.mintzbaptist.com/abc.shtml

The Carpenter's Story. Retrieved from
    http://www.coachingtohappiness.com/happiness-book/the-
    carpenters-story.html

The Five Finger Prayer. Retrieved from
    http://inspire21.com/stories/faithstories/TheFiveFingerPrayer

Thurman, H. Empowered Quote. Retrieved from
    http://empoweredquotes.com/c/quotations/empowerment-quotes/

Unknown. (n.d.). Comfort Zone. Retrieved from
    http://inspire21.com/stories/poetrystories/ComfortZone

Valvano, J. Retrieved from
http://www.brainyquote.com/quotes/authors/j/jim_valvano.html#p
ybhhCAku5ZtMc1I.99

http://www.brainyquote.com/quotes/keywords/compromise_4.html#RR6le
Zkzx3Y5W5RZ.99

Welles, J. Retrieved from http://EzineArticles.com/2216343

Willamson, M. Quote. Retrieved from
http://en.wikiquote.org/wiki/Marianne_Williamson

Wilson, C. Retrieved from http://effortandattitude.org/

Wintle, W. D. (n.d.). The Man Who Thinks He Can. Retrieved from
http://inspire21.com/stories/poetrystories/TheManWhoThinksHeC
an

Ziglar, Z. Retrieved from
http://thinkexist.com/quotation/winning_is_not_everything-
but_the_effort_to_win/145458.html

About the Author

Garrett has spent the last decade of his life devoting his time and efforts in assisting and motivating others to follow their dreams, specifically, through educational obtainment. He was born and raised in Greensburg, KY and resides in Elizabethtown, KY. His educational background consist of, BS in Organizational Leadership from the University of Louisville and an MA in Organizational Leadership from Campbellsville University. During that same time frame, he has worked in College Admissions and currently works as a College and Career Counselor, serves in the Air National Guard, and is an Ordained Minister. During his free time, you can find him with his wife and son, family and friends, working in the yard landscaping or participating in some other venture.

If you or your organization would like to schedule a speaking engagement or if you would like to follow Garrett you may do so via the following avenues:

Email: milbyg@hotmail.com
Facebook: /garrett.milby
Twitter: @garrettmilby

I want to personally thank you for taking the time to read Born to L.E.A.D: Leveraging Efforts and Attitudes into Dreams. It is my hope that you gained something from this twenty-eight day journey and I hope you will reference the materials often for motivation and guidance throughout life.

God Bless You,

Garrett. W. Milby

www.ingramcontent.com/pod-product-compliance
Lightning Source LLC
Chambersburg PA
CBHW060119050426
42448CB00010B/1948